ARMAND VAN DORMAEL

HEINZ NIXDORF

A GERMAN COMPUTER PIONEER

ARMAND VAN DORMAEL

HEINZ NIXDORF
A GERMAN COMPUTER PIONEER

ISBN: 1480155721
ISBN-13: 9781480155725

1 The Early Years

Heinz Nixdorf was born on April 9, 1925, in Paderborn, Germany. He was the son of Walter and Anne Nixdorf and the oldest of five children. His father, a traveling salesman, lost his job at the depth of the Depression. During the war, he was recruited for railway service. In 1944, he was killed when his train was blown up by Polish resistance fighters, thus plunging the family once more into distress. As the eldest son, Heinz helped support the family by working long hours on a nearby farm. These childhood experiences left an indelible mark.

Heinz at 6   *Heinz at 12*
Pictures courtesy of Nixdorf ComputerMuseumsForum.

At 14, he graduated from elementary school, scoring very high grades. His mother wanted him to become a teacher because it meant the guarantee of a secure career. She enrolled him in a boarding school in Konstanz, far away from home. Compelled to follow strict rules and regulations, the boy was very unhappy. He wrote a letter to the Ministry of Education in Berlin, explaining that he wanted to become a physicist rather than a teacher.

In 1943, after graduation, he was called up for military service. Stationed in Czechoslovakia, the division in which he served was wiped out. He survived and worked his way back to Paderborn. Now he was able to catch up with the schooling he had missed, and to prepare for his Abitur. A scholarship allowed him to attend the Reismann-Gymnasium in Paderborn, where he was noted as a highly gifted student with a special aptitude for mathematics. His teachers were impressed by his exceptional ability in analytical thinking and by his competitive spirit. In 1947, another scholarship allowed him to enroll in the Johann-Wolfgang-Goethe University in Frankfurt, where he studied physics and mathematics. He also took a course in business management.

Since his mother was unable to pay tuition fees, in order to fund his studies he took a job at the Frankfurt subsidiary of Remington Rand. There his life took an unforeseen turn when he met Dr. Walter Sprick, a data processing expert who ran the company's development laboratory. The 42-year old physicist experimented with automatic symbol identification of electronic adding machines and computer technology. Between 1949 and 1951, he had built an electronic calculator at the University of Kiel. The machine was connected to a Remington Rand card punching machine and had been installed at a savings bank. The device was not only smaller, but much more powerful than the machines sold by IBM and other manufacturers.

The director of the company visualized the potential; he asked him to develop a similar calculator and invited him to move to Frankfurt. Sprick accepted and set to work. But he needed assistance for his project, and was looking for two students capable of providing the necessary help. He contacted one of his friends who recommended Heinz Nixdorf as an extremely intelligent and ambitious young man. For the hourly wage of one DM, he put him to work. With incredible enthusiasm and insatiable curiosity, the young student immersed himself in his job, thus acquiring basic knowledge of electronic technology. But the project was abandoned when the management was given instructions by the US head office to put an end to it.

Nixdorf and friends at Frankfurt University in 1950.

Nixdorf was disappointed, but an idea germinated in his mind: IBM and Remington Rand were selling mainframe computers which were accessible only to very large corporations. Small and medium businesses could only afford electromechanical machines to perform multiplication and division by repetitive addition and subtraction. He was convinced that there was a vast and unexplored market for small electronic calculators. Electromechanical machines were very expensive because they required manual assembly. By replacing handcrafted wiring with mass-produced integrated circuits, the size of the machine would be much smaller and production costs considerably reduced.

Large corporations would also be interested: instead of a centrally operated accounting system which required paperwork to be moved from one office to the other, each department would perform the operations by itself. He tried to convince his mentor to set up a company together. But Sprick felt the risk was too great: he was 43, and the father of four children. Besides, he was a scientist and not a businessman.

Sprick was also convinced that German companies were not ready to buy electronic calculators. Their accounting departments were equipped with mechanical card punching machines. Most of these machines were leased by IBM who ensured their maintenance. Customers were not allowed to make any modifications or to connect any device produced by another company. IBM was in constant contact with its customers, which allowed its engineers to learn about their problems and wishes, and to develop improvements.

But Sprick's decision had another motive. The German subsidiary of IBM had offered him a well-paid lifetime job. He was given a free hand to conduct his research as he wished. He accepted, and stayed with the company until retirement. Disappointed, Heinz Nixdorf decided to go it alone. Sprick promised to give him every possible support whenever needed, and authorized him to make use of all the technical information contained in his patent. Convinced that he would able to build an electronic calculator all by himself, Heinz returned to Paderborn.[1]

2 His first Calculators

On June 30, 1952, Heinz Nixdorf registered the company name 'Labor für Impulstechnik'. His capital consisted of an idea, a few books, a moped and some hand tools. He made a list of the companies that might be interested in his project and toured the region on his moped. On several occasions he was not allowed beyond the porter's gate. When he succeeded in meeting a manager and tried to explain the purpose of his visit, none of them understood what he had in mind. After several unsuccessful calls, he tried his luck at the Rheinisch-Westfälische Elektrizitätswerke (RWE), Germany's largest electric power supplier.

He was introduced to the head of the punch card department, Mr. Lüking, who seemed interested. Lüking wanted to keep abreast of technical progress and patiently listened to what the young man had to say. He was impressed by his enthusiasm and his ability to convince. He realized that the use of small electronic calculators would expedite the workload of the accounting department and result in substantial cost savings. But Nixdorf was unable to produce a finished product and the engineering designs Moreover, the patents belonged to Walter Sprick.

Lüking talked the matter over with the director responsible for finance and auditing who was very skeptical. During the conversation, Nixdorf had mentioned that Sprick had installed an automatic calculator at a bank located in Kiel. He decided to have a look at the machine and came back with a very positive report. Thanks to this, he obtained the approval to go ahead with the project.

Nixdorf estimated that the construction of an electronic multiplier would cost about DM 30000. It was a lot of money and did not even include the expense of adapting it to a punchcard machine. Tentatively, and with reservations, the management approved, but not without safeguards. Lüking was given the green light on the condition that Walter Sprick agreed to vouch financially for his former student. When he gave the required guarantee, the cashier gave permission to proceed and made DM 5000 available. The young entrepreneur could finally start working.

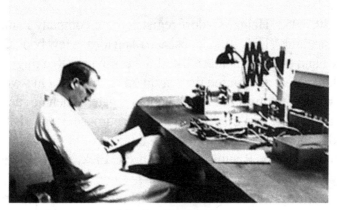

Nixdorf in 1952.

It was obvious that he would not be able to do the job alone and would need a well-trained, technically skilled assistant. At the store where he bought his supplies, he met Alfred Wierzoich, a radio and fax engineer who was intrigued by the project. When he visited the workshop RWE was making available, he decided to switch jobs. Thanks to his personal connections, material procurement became easy. The two young men set to work night and day. The RWE cashier only supplied additional funds when they proved that that they were making progress.

Based on Spricks' blueprints and ideas, they used radio tubes and other standard parts; but they also had to fabricate a vast number of electronic components and mechanical devices. Many of the parts had to be made by hand. For this, Nixdorf hired five more mechanics. It took more than a year to complete the first machine. Like the calculator developed by Sprick, it could add, subtract and multiply; but the RWE wanted a four-function device that could also divide. It took several months to work out the problems.

ES12

Early in 1954, the first electronic calculator, the ES12, was ready for testing. The device was intended to be connected by pluggable cables to a punched card data retrieval system. Nixdorf tried in vain to connect it to the Remington Rand machine in use at RWE. Lüking approached IBM, but was turned down. He knew that a company established in Cologne, the Exacta Büromaschinen GmbH, had the exclusive distribution of the French *Compagnie des Machines Bull* whose punched card Gamma 3 would probably do the job. Hans Braun, the sales manager of Exacta, was intrigued by Nixdorf's ideas and enthusiastically agreed to help.

Lüking was authorized to advance DM 40000 for the purchase of the Bull machine. The problem seemed to be solved, but Bull's management refused to become involved in the project. The company had recently developed a computer that would sell for DM 300000. Nixdorf's low-priced machine would be a dangerous competitor. Hans Braun was disappointed; but he was also convinced there was a market for small electronic calculators and decided to use a different approach.

He asked Nixdorf to demonstrate his calculator to the Bull management. Nixdorf and Wierzoich packed the machine into a large bag and took the train to Cologne. The Bull people were so impressed by the demonstration that they not only agreed to sell the punch card machine, but decided to buy Nixdorf's calculator and sell it under their own brand.

At Bull's request, Nixdorf then developed the Gamma 10. It was a mixture between a classic punch card machine and a modern computer. It had a huge number of small relays, a plugboard, a very fast card reader and a puncher, transistorized logic and three different types of core memory.

The standard equipment featured a CPU with panel, a punch card reader/puncher unit and a barrel printer. The RAM consisted of a 1kb core memory which could be extended up to 4kb capacity. The cycle time from the core memory was 7 microseconds. The calculator was capable of reading and punching 300 cards per minute.

Inside View of Bull Gamma10.

It was a huge success and gave Exacta a new start. The finance department of Germany's largest federal state, Nordrhein-Westfalen, placed a substantial order. For Nixdorf this meant that more personnel and larger premises were urgently needed. A large building located on the RWE grounds was equipped with the necessary machinery; more people were hired.[2]

Within a few months, Nixdorf developed an electronic multiplier the EM20. Coupled to a punch card machine, it allowed banks to automatically perform various operations. It was an instant success and gave Bull a technical and commercial advantage over IBM. In France and Germany, a vast number of banks adopted the system. By the same token, it allowed Exacta to considerably improve its image and gave Nixdorf the opportunity to familiarize himself with the needs of the banking industry.

By 1957, the Labor für Impulstechnik employed 27 people. Nixdorf urgently needed a new technical director. He recognized that the vacuum tube was obsolete and had to be replaced as quickly as possible by transistors. He contacted a Dutch engineer, Jan van Koppen, who worked at Philips in Eindhoven and was familiar with semiconductor technology. Fascinated by the enterprising spirit of the young entrepreneur, he decided to move to Paderborn. Nixdorf gave him a substantial salary and a new Opel-Kapitän.

Alfred Wierzoich, the man of the first hour, felt like being hit on the head. He wanted to continue his laboratory work and develop new products. But Nixdorf assigned him to customer service and machine maintenance. For a few months, he toured the region with his old Volkswagen, but finally decided to give up and leave.

Nixdorf's sales kept growing at a fast pace. The chairman of Exacta, Hans Bringer, gave him his full support. Once more, additional personnel and equipment were needed. Finding a suitable site an affordable price was not easy. Fortunately, the city council of Paderborn put an empty building at his disposal. Nixdorf was also able to buy at low cost a piece of land; within a year he moved into a building that was his property. Meanwhile, the number of employees had increased to 104 and the turnover reached nearly DM 7 million.

In 1958, Exacta completed the development of the Multitronic 6000. The project had been very costly and had taken up much time. When it finally came on the market, it did not sell because it was too slow. Nixdorf suggested the replacement of vacuum tubes by transistors; it was an immediate success. But another problem was lurking: IBM and Remington Rand were conquering new markets with smaller and less expensive computers. The era of electronic calculators and punch card machines was coming to an end; new and technically more advanced calculators were needed. Sprick's patents had become useless.

Nixdorf needed someone with new and original ideas, capable of developing a machine that would be ahead of competition. The problem was to find the right man. He recalled that in May 1963, at the Hannover Fair, he had been very much intrigued by a calculator shown at the AEG-Telefunken booth and called TR 10. It was the smallest machine he had ever seen.

On close examination of the inside, he discovered another peculiarity: the wiring of the boards was not the usual tangled mess, but was installed in parallel, which facilitated maintenance and repair. He tried to locate the man who had developed the machine and was told that his name was Otto Müller who worked at the IBM Research Center in Yorktown Heights.

The 39-year-old engineer had been part of the team that built the AEG-Telefunken TR 440. He had been allowed to spend most of the time all by himself on the development of a small computer which he called TR 10. His wife had a job as an accountant; she complained about the chore of tedious manual work she had to put up with and suggested that he develop a small machine to automatically create invoices and calculate payroll.

He had been thinking about the advantages of small electronic calculators and about their potential: the cost of production would be a fraction of the expense involved in building a mainframe; a vast number of the mechanical components could be replaced by a micro program that was easily duplicated at little expense.

The head of the project felt it was a waste of time, but let him pursue his idea. The machine was exhibited at the Hannover Fair in 1962, but did not attract any attention; the general feeling was that there existed no market for small calculators.

Disappointed, and out of sheer anger, Müller handed in his resignation. Since nobody was interested in Germany, he decided to try his luck in the United States. He sent a letter to the personnel manager of IBM in Yorktown Heights, explaining that he had developed a small computer and would like to submit his project. He was hired and obtained permission to prepare blueprints and specifications for the hardware and the software, and documentation about how the calculator would be constructed.

When Müller submitted the specifications of the program he had developed, he was told that IBM was not interested in the construction of a prototype because a small office computer did not fit within the concept and the program of the company. Once more, frustrated and discouraged, he was brooding about his future, when he received a letter from Germany. In a few lines, Nixdorf mentioned that on his recent visit to the Hannover Fair he had been impressed by the TR10. He wanted to develop a new calculator and was looking for an engineer with interesting ideas. Two airplane tickets were included with the letter.

Müller was thrilled: this finally gave him the opportunity to build the computer he had in mind. Within a few days, he was in Paderborn. He realized that his decision to change jobs was not without risk. He was leaving the research laboratory of the world's largest and most famous computer manufacturer for the laboratory of a small and unknown startup. But the opportunity to complete the project he had in mind was simply more important. Besides, his boss at IBM had left open his way back.

Upon his arrival, he found Nixdorf in a state of perplexity and anxiety. He urgently needed a new calculator, but was unable to decide which one he should choose. Müller's project seemed interesting, but he was not sure that the man could do what he promised. His project was based on a new and untried technology, and its realization would require substantial development costs of which the outcome was uncertain. If necessary, he could count on Hager and Hahnewinkel who had developed several improved models. But he did not know to what extent micro-programmed control would work better than hardware control and feared that he might be heading towards a fiasco. For the first time, Nixdorf felt undecided and insecure.

But time was pressing and he decided it was safer to let Hager and Hahnewinkel go ahead, and to defer any other project. Deeply shocked, Müller went to see his wife who was at the local hospital in the maternity ward. She listened to what he had to say and decided to intervene. The day she was released from hospital, she went to see Nixdorf and put him before the alternative: either he made up his mind within two weeks and let her husband build his computer, or he will resign and go back to IBM. She even went to say that he would work without pay until the day he produced a working computer. Moved and impressed, Nixdorf agreed to let him go ahead. It took Müller eight months to complete the machine.

In May 1965, at the Hannover Fair, the booths of Wanderer and Ruf displayed four computers. Except for the name, they were identical. Three of them were called the Nixdorf 820. The Wanderer management gave it the name Logatronic.[3]

Nixdorf 820.

The 820 was the world's first program-controlled office computer. It attracted a lot of attention and was an instant success. Mainframe computers still dominated, but the office equipment industry was in the midst of upheaval. The industry leader, IBM, had clearly staked out its position. Siemens, AEG and the other German office equipment manufacturers were searching for ways to capture a share of the market. Captives of a long and successful tradition of mechanical engineering, they were reluctant to break with the past. Nixdorf was a newcomer. He started out with an unbeatable asset: he had learned from Sprick that the only way to make small calculators was to replace the mechanical parts by electronic relays.

The Nixdorf 820 had a threaded ROM which was programmable. Thus the electronic calculator became a computer. The console consisted of a typewriter, a magnetic account reader and two punch card readers. In addition, the system supported a punch card unit, a high speed matrix printer, two cassette tape drives and a stand-alone card puncher.

Threaded ROM

Unlike conventional calculators, the output and input devices such as writing and printing were not controlled by hardware components, but by a software program. In mainframe computers, micro-program control was still stuck in its very early stages. More important, the 820 was constructed on the modular principle; its production costs were only a fraction of the devices available on the market. The basic system was later equipped with magnetic ledger card facilities for storing data, a dot matrix printer and a module that permitted data to be transferred to higher-level computers. This enabled Nixdorf to produce a series of machines with a decisive technical superiority at a very significant cost advantage. It resulted in a competitive advantage that would keep him for years ahead of competition.

The 820 marked the beginning of the shift from centralized to decentralized data processing. For the first time, small and medium-sized businesses were able to process their financial accounting and inventory data electronically. At a stroke, Wanderer's financial problems seemed to vanish. The 820 gave Nixdorf the opportunity to break out of anonymity. For him, it meant a new start.[4]

3 The Nixdorf 820

In the mid-1960s few people envisaged any but IBM's concept of computer utilization, in which ever-larger central processing units handled a growing amount of corporate data from a single location. Heinz Nixdorf was convinced that most companies did not need that much computational muscle; they needed small machines that were easy to operate and maintain. In fact, they required two elements IBM was not interested in supplying: small, versatile computers and a sales force able to tailor such machines to the specific needs of each customer. This strategy was not only sound; it also addressed the realities of the West German economy, whose companies tended to be smaller outfits. Many of them were family-owned concerns unable to invest in a mainframe or a minicomputer, but still in need of computing efficiency. For these customers Nixdorf brought out the 820. He also organized a sales force and a maintenance service ready to adapt each machine to the needs of the client.

At the opening day of the 1968 Hannover Fair, Heinz Nixdorf made the headlines. The newspapers announced that he had bought Wanderer. All of a sudden, the owner of a small and unknown company presented himself as an independent computer manufacturer in a market dominated by large corporations. People wanted to know what he had to offer. His inconspicuous fair stand was located in the booth of Wanderer and Ruf, which displayed four machines. Except for the name, they were identical. The Wanderer management named it Logatronic; Kienzle and Ruf, marketed it under the brand Digitronic. The Nixdorf 820 was the world's first micro-program-controlled minicomputer, tailored to small-and medium sized enterprises.

The Nixdorf 820.

The 820 was a fully programmable minicomputer with magnetic core memory, a built-in keyboard and a typewriter for data output. It established Nixdorf's reputation as the pioneer of decentralized data processing. The basic system was later equipped with a magnetic data storage account, a dot matrix printer and a module that allowed data transfer to higher level computers.

The booth was beset from morning till evening by a vast crowd of onlookers and potential buyers who were surprised and impressed by the fact that a young entrepreneur had the nerve to challenge the giants of the industry. All of a sudden, an unknown office machine manufacturer who used to supply other companies presented himself as an independent producer, determined to enter a market dominated by big names. The young entrepreneur now not only had his own production facilities, but his own distribution setup.

The Nixdorf 820 was a world premiere. Not only did it create a sensation; it was from the start a huge commercial success. Unlike conventional electronic computers, the output and input devices, such as writing and printing, were not controlled by hardware components, but by a built-in program. Until then, micro-program control was only available in large computers. It had been used for some time, but was still in its early stages.

The Nixdorf 820 used rod cell read-only memory to store its operating system. Also called magnetic stick memory, this technology featured a board studded with 144 vertical rods of wire coil. If one of its 256 hand-threaded wires went around a rod, it represented a one; threaded past a rod, it represented a zero.

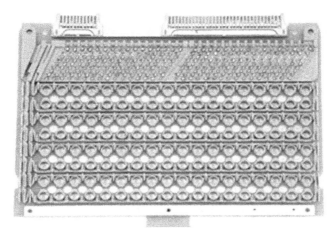

Rod Cell Memory Board.

Even more important, the Nixdorf 820 was constructed on the modular principle. Its production cost represented only a fraction of devices with comparable features. Its micro-program control system was much faster and more powerful than the smallest computer made by IBM. He thus not only had a product that was technically superior, but also had a very significant cost advantage. The 820 marked the beginning of the shift from centralized to decentralized data processing. For the first time, it enabled small and medium-sized businesses to process their financial accounting and inventory data electronically at very reasonable cost.[5]

Money could thus be used for research and development and for the acquisition of machinery and equipment. Although Nixdorf s computers were by far the lowest priced, his benefit-cost ratio was so favorable that it allowed him to make substantial profits. Even more important, the acquisition of Wanderer gave him a well-staffed sales organization.

The huge losses incurred by Wanderer in 1966 and 1967, turned out to be a blessing. German tax law allowed to offset current financial years' operating losses against the income earned the preceding year.

Dr. Hermann Karoli had been for more than 20 years Nixdorf's advisor dealing with the company's financing and taxation. He devised a seemingly straightforward and almost inconspicuous scheme that ultimately achieved a surprising effect. The Wanderer shares were taken over by Nixdorf s wife. The capital base was increased from DM 7.5 million to DM 30 million. To finalize the operation, the company was renamed Nixdorf Computer AG. The result was surprising: despite huge profits, taxes were close to nil.

From now on, Nixdorf's only goal was to keep growing. But the takeover of Wanderer was not without problems. The company faced tremendous challenges and urgently needed a fundamental reorganization. The issues were complicated by the fact that Nixdorf refused to associate with the Wanderer people. Their corporate governance was different; their way of thinking and their ethics did not comply with his own standards. His aversion was largely due to the memory of his angry confrontations with Otto Budde and his successor Albert Greiner, who not only threatened him with legal proceedings, but tried to blackmail him by insinuating they might copy his calculators instead of buying them. This had left feelings of disgust and anger in his mind. For quite some time, he refused to visit the Cologne plant.

But the company needed new management. He appointed Hans Bringer as chairman; Hans Braun was made responsible for the reorganization, while Helmut Rausch took care of sales. Their first task was to find a way to clean up the mess in which the company was embroiled. It was also urgent to spell out a program that would allow both companies to work together.

The first opportunity arose when the Paderborn plant was unable to respond to a sudden increase in demand for the Nixdorf 820. Cologne could have stepped in; but Nixdorf had no confidence and feared that they might deliver substandard quality equipment and jeopardize the reputation of the 820. He wanted to expand as quickly as possible the Paderborn production facilities and develop a network of local sales and service offices. This meant increased competition for Cologne. He decided that Paderborn would supply the banking industry and large corporations, while Cologne would focus on small and medium-sized customers. Five years after the acquisition of Wanderer, Nixdorf employed about 7000 people. The company had grown from a development and production operation to a full-fledged industrial corporation.

EMBED StaticMetafile
The Nixdorf 820 with punch card machine and printer.

The decade of the 1970s was the most productive in the history of the company. During this period, Nixdorf became the market leader in Germany in the field of data systems technology and the fourth largest computer manufacturer in Europe, with production facilities in Germany, Ireland, Spain, the United States and Singapore. In 1975, its engineers completed the development of a new generation of data acquisition and data processing systems plus a vast range of electronic cash registers and self-banking terminals. Another sector included the area of data acquisition systems using electromagnetic tape in replacement of punch cards. In 1978, on the 25th anniversary of the company, sales exceeded for the first time DM 1 billion.

Since 1973, despite rising profits, the Nixdorf Computer AG hardly paid any taxes. Following the marketing strategy adopted by the computer industry, he had decided to enter the rental business. He realized that he could gain substantially more customers among small and medium-sized enterprises, if he gave them the opportunity to lease the machines instead of buying them.

For the lessee, the benefits of leasing vs. purchasing were obvious: instead of the full price, payments are made by installments; lease payments can be deducted as business expenses; leasing minimizes the impact on the budget since the customer pays only for the use of the equipment; payment structures can be tailored to fit the clients' specific needs; at the end of the contract the customer can return the equipment, purchase it or extend the agreement. Leasing gives better protection against technology obsolescence and the opportunity to buy new software in order to take advantage of the latest technology developments.

For Nixdorf the benefits were substantial: his customers were entitled to a new computer or to a machine that performed exactly like it; the lease was coupled with maintenance agreement; if a customer did not pay the full rent, the machine was recuperated; the property remained on the balance sheet and was depreciated over time; for accounting purposes the transaction was treated as though the lessor had granted the lessee a loan to purchase the asset; the lessee undertook all the risks of ownership; at the end of each contract, the computers were returned to the factory to be refurbished and brought up-to-date.

Together with the Westdeutsche Landesbank, Nixdorf founded the Nixdorf Computer Miete KG. He owned 55 percent of the shares, while the bank was involved with 45 percent. In order to finance the transaction process and to assure the cash flow, the bank opened a credit line of DM 500 million. This gave him a substantial financial flexibility. Since the lending company was a separate corporation, its earnings report did not have to be consolidated with the profit and loss statement of the Nixdorf Computer AG.

An aggressive marketing campaign resulted in the explosive increase of the lease contracts; more than 80 percent of the computers were marketed this way. In the balance sheet of the company, the rentals were reported as sales, whereas in reality they were loans financed on credit. According to the accounting standards of German law this was a permissible procedure. The profits realized by the Nixdorf Computer Miete KG constituted a godsend in the 1973-75 crisis years.[6]

During the 1970s Nixdorf continued to defy conventional wisdom by exploiting the niche he had uncovered. The company's first international sales operations were conducted in Sweden. They provided the Swedish banking industry with 1000 terminals. By 1972, Nixdorf had opened sales centers in 21 countries. In the mid-seventies, the press continued to publish stories about the amazing accomplishments of the Nixdorf Computer AG. In an interview he had stated: "Our sales exceed one percent of the global computer market, and we are among the twelve largest companies in the industry". And he added that in 1975 sales would exceed one billion DM. But in Paderborn, behind closed doors a mood of uncertainty, concern and nervousness prevailed.

In fact, he had to contend with several challenges. The dollar crisis of 1971 had thrown the European economy into recession and reduced the demand for office equipment. But his main problem was of a different nature. The 820 developed in 1965 by Otto Müller had become outdated . Although it had been improved again and again, it was being overtaken by competition and responded no more to the needs and expectations of the customers. It was urgent to decide whether the time had come to draw a line and stop production. So far, he had been able to prolong the life by making gradual improvements. If he decided on a new product, he had to make sure it would be equally successful.

Müller was working on a more powerful system. He had conceived a freely programmable computer with integrated screen and cassette memory. But Nixdorf did not quite understand what he had in mind and paid no attention. He was confronted by another problem in the development laboratory: Hahnewinkel, Hager and Bonatschek were at loggerheads with each other. Instead of working like a team on a common project, they tried to outdo one another, each pursuing his own ideas. Their quarrels became from day to day more insufferable.

Nixdorf shrank away from taking a stand; but his arguments with Müller increasingly led to an inevitable break. Lise Müller, convinced to act in the interest of both men, tried to soften things up. But Nixdorf felt he was at the mercy of an insufferably stubborn engineer and his ambitious wife. In December 1978, following a dispute between the two men, Müller resigned. His departure freed Nixdorf from an oppressive dependence and solved a personal problem. But he took the risk of creating a vacuum in the product development program that would be difficult to fill. He suddenly faced the dilemma of having to decide whether to draw a line under the success story of the 820 or to continue upgrading until this was no longer technically feasible.

If he decided to launch a new model, where would it come from? Helmut Rausch made a trip to the United States hoping to find a suitable new product. He discovered that a small American computer manufacturer, called Entrex, had developed a radically innovative data collection process. Instead of punch cards for input, processing and data storage, the system ran on magnetic tape and magnetic disks. It consisted of a central unit with hard disk and tape station. Terminals could be used up to 64. Within a short time, thanks to this new program, Nixdorf supplied almost half of the machines sold in Germany to become the leading provider of data collection systems in Europe, with a market share of 24 percent.

The yearly growth rates of more than 20 percent gave the company a new dimension. By 1978, its share of the European office equipment market increased to 27 percent, which made it the number one supplier. The pace of rapid growth continued for several years. The success of the 820 proved that Nixdorf had made the right choice by betting on the potential of individual workstations. The market proved to be much more important than he expected.

Whereas the 820 was originally intended for small and large businesses, the larger corporations soon came to appreciate its advantages. It amply served most of their needs at a fraction of the costs of buying and running a mainframe or a minicomputer.

A computer costing several million DM made access to the technology possible only to a few large corporations. Whereas the industry kept building larger and faster computers, Nixdorf opened a new market. Since his customers had no experience in the use of computers and could not afford an expert, he set up a large maintenance and servicing department able to assure maximum customer satisfaction.

Next to the concept of bringing the computer to the workplace, his decision to develop a range of software programs adapted to the needs of each type of customer was another secret for his success. He became the largest software producer in Europe. More than a fifth of the workforce was engaged in the development, distribution and consulting. This gave him a tremendous competitive advantage. In the market of data processing for banking terminals, Nixdorf was able to successfully assert himself against the market leaders.

The 820 was the first bank terminal with integrated data processing. German savings banks were his first customers. From 1978, this business experienced an enormous upswing. Four years later, 40000 computers had been installed. In 1982, almost half of the largest European banks were Nixdorf customers. With a market share of more than 40 percent, the company became by far the largest provider of peripheral terminals for financial institutions.

Based on a proven and successful program of terminals and mid-size computers, Nixdorf strengthened the company's position in the market. Within a few years, the workforce doubled from 10000 to 20000 employees.

But suddenly, the global economy slid into a deep recession. The demand for office equipment dropped. During the years of fast growth, the major European office equipment manufacturers - Olivetti, Philips, Ericsson, Triumph-Adler and Kienzle had vastly expanded their production. IBM, which until then had focused exclusively on the mainframe business, had entered the market with its low-end System 32 intended to meet the needs of small and medium businesses. It all led to fierce competition for every customer.

In the late 1960s, the major computer manufacturers increasingly faced unforeseen competition. Minicomputers captured a larger share of the market. The development of integrated circuits and core memory technologies allowed a growing number of small and medium companies to enter the market of the big ones. They were successful because their small machines were much cheaper than the mainframes.

Their computers were built for limited use, but they met the practical needs of most companies as well, and sometimes better, than the huge computers used by the large corporations. The market had changed and he was exposed to increasing competition. The personal computer was on the rise. The brand loyalty of the typical Nixdorf customer who relied on the personal services of the company began to fade. The product life cycle of the 8870 was coming to its inevitable end. Nixdorf did not want to get involved in the development of a standard MS-DOS personal computer.

For several years, an unspoken agreement led to a price discipline that was observed as a law. The 'Seven Dwarfs' aligned their prices with those of IBM. Nobody would have dared enter into a price war with the market leader. Their huge profit margins were justified by the argument that the high development costs had to be amortized and were needed for future research. The upstarts producing midrange computers benefited from three decades of research and development. For the major companies a competitive battle was very inopportune. It was expected that for the next few years sales would not increase by more than ten percent. In the field of low-priced computers, the boom in Europe was still to come.[7]

4 A One-Man Global Company

The takeover of Wanderer confronted the new management with the arduous task of having to restructure the company and to decide on a manufacturing program that would solve its numerous problems. It was also urgent to develop a common understanding of the way both factory systems could be made complementary. In Cologne, manufacturing focused on mechanical calculators, but production capacity was largely unused.

While management was brooding over a seemingly hopeless situation, a telex from Chicago opened a whole new perspective. In August 1968, the president of Victor Comptometer Corporation announced that he had seen reports about the Conti, and was intrigued by the fact that it was the first electronic printing calculator. He was interested in a license agreement, and needed information about the technical specifications and the manufacturing processes. He wanted to know how much the package would cost.

Victor was a highly diversified family-owned company and the world's largest manufacturer of calculators. After a series of meetings, it was agreed that Victor would have the sole distribution rights for the United States and Canada. Shortly after, it came as an overwhelming surprise when Victor placed an order for 10000 machines. Production capacity of the Cologne plant was limited to 50 units a week; this meant that new personnel had to be hired.

The Conti was rebadged Victor 1500. The company launched a costly advertising campaign, expecting to open a new market for small business machines. After a brief success, sales turned out to be disappointing. The US computer market was structured differently. In Europe, the secret of Nixdorf s success was due to the fact that he brought small computers to the individual workplace. This did not reflect the centralist organization prevailing in the United States, where corporate input and output data were performed through central processing units installed in a single location, which users tapped into from remote keyboards. Nobody envisaged any but IBM's concept of computer utilization, in which ever-larger central processing units handled a growing amount of corporate data from a single location.[8]

After an initial success, sales of the Conti suddenly dropped. Nixdorf had foreseen that this would happen. The contract was not terminated, but the expansion of the sales organization had strained the financial strength of Victor. In 1972, the management decided to sell its computer division. An agreement was made whereby Victor took over the US distributorship of the 820. Nixdorf now achieved what he really wanted: a distributorship by a company familiar with the US market. It soon turned out to be a bitter disappointment. The structure of the US market was very different from the German and European environment.

But Nixdorf considered the American market an essential part of his overall strategy. His exceptional growth in Europe augured well for his success in the United States. Sales of his own products would probably be limited, but a presence across the Atlantic would give him opportunities for making contacts and acquire new and successful ideas and products. The venture was a gamble worthwhile trying, even if setbacks had to be expected. Eager to play an important part in the international computer business, he was ready for the experience.

From the beginning, Nixdorf considered the venture as a stepping stone to gain access to the American market. He was convinced that, in order to compete effectively with US companies in the long run, he had to learn how they competed among themselves. It was the only way to avoid being ultimately swept over in his home market. In this game, product innovation played a crucial role.[9]

This gave him what he had wanted from the beginning, namely a distributor who knew the US market. The managers of Victor threw themselves with enthusiasm into this new venture; but it soon became evident that the venture would result in heavy losses. In 1971, sales amounted to $ 11 million with an operating loss of $ 2 million.

In November 1972, Nixdorf acquired the computer activities of Victor for $ 10 million. Within a few days, he registered the Nixdorf Computer Inc. and set up a production facility in Schaumburg, near Chicago. Within four years, about 3000 machines were installed. Employment had risen to 1000 people and the sales and service network was expanded to 30 cities. [10]

Having established a bridgehead in the United States, Nixdorf decided to be on the lookout for a new series of machines the company urgently needed, but was unable to produce. The departure of Otto Müller had created a gap in product development projects that was hard to fill. This situation arose at a moment when the company was confronted with the complex issue of having to decide whether or not the time had come to draw a line under the success of the 820 and to launch a new line of calculators.

On a visit to the United States, Helmut Rausch discovered that a small American computer manufacturer called Entrex, had developed an interactive data collection system. It consisted of a central processing unit with hard disk and magnetic tape instead of punched cards. It could be connected to 64 terminals and promised to open up an interesting market niche. Nixdorf concluded a license agreement with Entrex.

In 1973, the 620 system was introduced to the market. It was the company's first major success with a product purchased outside. Within a relatively short time, Nixdorf became the leading provider of data collection systems, capturing a market share of 24 percent in Europe and 45 percent in Germany. Very soon, the Paderborn engineers developed a new range of programs based on the 620. It became the basis of a broad line of that made Nixdorf a leading provider of software program. Not content with the license agreement he had signed with Entrex, he negotiated the takeover the company and integrated it within the computer division of Victor. In May 1977, Nixdorf acquired Entrex for $ 22 million. It was the most important step in the development of the company's international operations.

In 1975, he set up a new production facility in Schaumburg, near Chicago. By now, about 3000 systems had been installed. Employment had risen to 1000 people; the sales and service network had been expanded to 130 cities. Finally completed the acquisition A few months later, Entrex was completely integrated into Nixdorf Computer Corp.[10]

Thanks to the acquisition of Entrex, Nixdorf doubled his dollar volume in the United States. At a press conference in New York, he spelled out his plans for the future: "The presence in the world's largest computer market is the most the most important prerequisite for long-term business success in the computer business .The acquisition price of Entrex represented an investment of $ 22 million. ..The number of employees in the United States would be increased to more than and service personnel would operate in more than 130 locations. Entrex would gradually be integrated into the Nixdorf Computer Inc.[11]

More than ever, Nixdorf was convinced that the best way to establish his presence in the United States market was to cooperate with small companies whose engineers had developed products that incorporated cut-rate technology. "A European computer company can only assure long-term competitiveness in the global market through technological cooperation with American companies. Our research activities are mainly aimed at the direct support of operations on individual jobs by using the data processing capabilities of the decentralized, task-related use of computers to reach" With the acquisition of the Entrex data collection system 620, for the first time since 1973, Nixdorf entered the market with a new product for the next generation of computers.

In 1976, Nixdorf increased his activities abroad. The sales organization in Scandinavia was restructured. The operations in Denmark, Norway and Sweden were transferred to Logtron, a subsidiary of the Danish Bording Group, In Ireland, Nixdorf built a new production facility in the vicinity of Dublin.

The takeover of Victor Computer and Entrex gave Nixdorf a foothold in the U.S. market. In March 1971, he achieved another spectacular coup: he signed a long-term agreement with Kanematsu-Gosho Ltd, the third-largest Japanese trading house. For quite some time, the management had wished to enter the computer business and searched in vain for a manufacturer willing to supply machines under a private brand. The president of the company, Gyota Machida was intrigued by Japanese press reports describing the exceptional characteristics of the Nixdorf 820 calculators. After initial contacts, Peter Ehrlich made a trip to Tokyo and came back home with an order for 5000 computers.

Nixdorf exulted. 'We are the first European computer company able to export to the United States and Japan', he said. While he was pleased with the success, he realized that he would be unable to conquer more than a small fraction of the Japanese market. Nevertheless, he considered that the close contact with Kanematsu-Gosho and Victor were of great strategic importance.

At a press conference, he stated: 'If we want to assert ourselves in the long run against our main competitors in the global computer market, we must learn to know how they operate at home. It is the only way we can avoid being unexpectedly rolled over in our own market. Product development plays a crucial role in our industry; that means we must watch competition and get as early as possible an insight into the product developments of our American and Japanese competitors.' Within a few months, Kanematsu-Gosho set up a distribution and service organization.[12]

Nixdorf decided time had come to expand his involvement in the Asian market and make it into the 'third pillar' of the group. He already had a small subsidiary in Singapore which employed 200 people. In 1986, he built a fully automated factory for the production of peripheral systems. For the next five years, he planned to invest $ 38 million in the project, thereby creating 750 jobs. The plant was to produce printer heads, keyboards, screen displays and electronic modules for assembly in Paderborn.[13]

5 A Huge Market for Small Computers

In 1965, when Nixdorf presented his 820 at the Hannover Fair, computer technology was accessible only to very large corporations, public utilities, government agencies and the military. They used mainframes to perform automatically a series of data processing operations, such as payroll, stock records, cost accounting, engineering and scientific research. IBM's 604, Remington Rand's 406-2 and Bull's Gamma 10 shared the European data processing market. Input and output data were processed through a computer installed at a single location which users tapped into from remote keyboards. Few people envisioned that computers could be conceived any other way.

Seven years after the end of the war, European office equipment manufacturers were still in the process of rebuilding plants and production capacity by redesigning their pre-war calculating machines. Nixdorf saw the opportunity to open up new markets based on a new technology. Unencumbered by the electromechanical tradition of the industry, he visualized the market potential of small electronic machines. In the mid-1960s, he introduced computers which, thanks to their price/performance ratio, were accessible to small and medium-sized enterprises. In line with his user-oriented approach, he provided demand-oriented software and computer training.

The computer industry was dominated by a few very large companies; he was convinced that the potential of small electronic calculators was immense. He opened new segments of the market and filled the needs and requirements of a vast number of companies that so far had been unable to afford a computer. Thanks to the 820, medium- and small companies had at their disposal a machine that allowed them to manage their invoicing, order processing, stock management and other accounts at a reasonable cost. Since these customers could not afford an expert to take care of the maintenance, he decided that with every machine he would provide extensive technical assistance.

This all-in service secured his company a competitive advantage and ensured an immediate success. He managed to maintain this lead with machines which, in the course of a few years, matured into multi-user systems in networks of their own or linked to mainframes. Twenty years before the advent of the personal computer, his concept of introducing electronic data processing to the workplace, pioneered decentralized computing. He revolutionized the market for mid-range computers and became the fourth largest computer manufacturer in Europe.

Computer manufacturers left it to their customers take care of the application problems. In the United States, companies used in-house resources to keep their computers running. Nixdorf Computer AG, with its extensive support, repair and troubleshooting services, had a definite advantage.

Personalized software was another secret of his success. He was the first to provide his customers with advice and technical solutions that covered most of their needs. For this, the company employed a staff of software developers. By 1970, Nixdorf employed 4800 people. The expansion had taken place without resorting to bank credit. He expected that his sales volume would continue to increase by 40 percent each year, and was convinced that he could finance this on his own. If necessary, he might sell part of his shares to a silent partner interested in the financial investment, but without participation in the management of the company. It would of course be very difficult to determine the market value of the shares. He was not interested in selling any of his stock; but he knew that in the long run it might be difficult to go it alone.

1968 was a banner year for Nixdorf and his company. He took over the Wanderer organization and set up the Nixdorf Computer AG. His sales volume exceeded DM 100 million. The company had 24 sales offices in Germany, 8 foreign subsidiaries and general agencies in 13 countries

He was no more an anonymous sub-tier supplier. Prior to the takeover of Wanderer, his direct sales business had been very limited and a very small staff had taken care of it: Helmut Rausch and Klaus Luft were in charge of domestic sales; William Ehrlich was made responsible for international activities.[14]

During the 1970s, Nixdorf continued to defy conventional wisdom by exploiting the niche he had uncovered. This phase of expansion was mainly due to the sales success of the Nixdorf computer 820. Since he launched it in 1967 as a general purpose computer, the machine had been further developed.

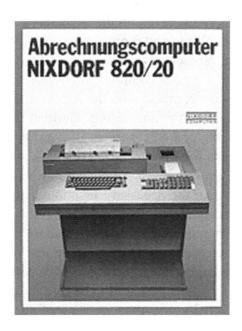

The explosive sales increases of the early seventies could not hide the fact that the company was no more in its most innovative period. For too long its success had rested on the 820. However, these machines, despite constant upgrading, no longer met the customers' needs; and an appropriately adapted successor was not in sight.

In addition, global economic conditions deteriorated rapidly. The years 1974 and 1975 were bad times for the computer industry.

Heinz Nixdorf described the situation as follows: "In 1974, we faced the consequences of the oil crisis and of the huge wage increases granted under the Brandt government, the doubling of the interest rate and the appreciation of the D-mark. Under the circumstances, I was forced to limit production." In fact, in 1974, he reduced the workforce from 8506 to 7954.

But, as if he had foreseen hard times, in the early seventies he set up a rental business, the Nixdorf Computer Miete KG. He owned 55 percent of the shares, while the Westdeutsche Landesbank subscribed 45 percent. The bank granted a loan of DM 300 million for expansion abroad. The operation did not have to be reported in the balance sheet. This credit gave him the necessary financial flexibility to be largely spared from capital problems.

But for a while, Nixdorf seemed to be out of luck. He had become convinced that the German computer manufacturers would, in the long run, be unable to compete with the Americans unless the industry was consolidated into a functioning 'German Union'.

In April 1970, he took a 20 percent in a group called Datel. The association had been founded by AEG-Telefunken, Siemens and the German Federal Post Office for the purpose of helping the data processing industry make the necessary technological breakthrough to remain globally competitive. It was the unanimous opinion of the founders that the project could ultimately lead to the development of a German computer system with a complete line of machines, from the smallest to the largest, each having its own software program. It did not take long for the experiment to be discontinued.

In December, 1978, the management of the Deutsche Bank announced that it had taken a substantial participation in the capital of Nixdorf Computer AG. For the first time, Nixdorf agreed to sell part of his shares. At a press conference, he made it clear that this would in no way affect his position. On all occasions and under every circumstance, he alone would make the important decisions; but to pursue the rapid expansion of his company, he needed additional capital. Starting from scratch, within a few years he ranked third in Germany with a market share of 6.4 percent.

In the field of data processing for banking terminals Nixdorf also took the lead. German savings banks were his first customers. His reputation in the banking sector took a new dimension in 1974, when he installed 1400 terminals at the Swedish Scandinaviska Enskilda-Bank, which operated branches throughout Sweden. The product range for financial institutions was extended in 1978 with the addition of self-service systems, such as statement printers and automated teller machines.

In January 1972, together with AEG Telefunken, Nixdorf founded the Telefunken Computer GmbH with headquarters in Konstanz. The Federal Ministry of Education and Research had granted a substantial subsidy. The purpose was the production and distribution of the AEG mainframe computer program. AEG-Telefunken had transferred its computer division to the new company. In addition, basic and application software, peripheral devices and document processing systems were part of the program. AEG- Telefunken had transferred its computer division to the new company, hoping that such cooperation would help to bring its data processing system to the market place. Nixdorf, on the other hand, envisioned that it would give him the leap into the mainframe business and become a counterweight to IBM and the other American companies.

The Konstanz venture was a flop. The Telefunken Computer GmbH never got out of the red, and the expected development of the computer system TR 440 did not come about. The government did not want to see money wasted any further and asked Siemens to take over the company. Since its inception, the Telefunken Computer GmbH had accumulated a loss of 86 million DM. Nixdorf came out of the venture with a black eye.

He decided to concentrate on the market potential of the 820, which seemed inexhaustible. In the five years since the takeover of Wanderer, Nixdorf had quintupled his sales to almost 500 million DM. The growth of the company had been phenomenal. Nixdorf was utterly optimistic and confident that further expansion was assured. In fact, behind its stolid facade, serious problems were building up.[15]

6 The 8870 Series

In the mid-seventies, the press continued to publish reports about the accomplishments and the expansion of the Nixdorf Computer AG. In an interview with the Frankfurter Rundschau, Nixdorf displayed unbridled optimism. As usual, he acted as ambassador for the company and was its number one salesman, showing self-confidence, even when problems threatened to grow over his head. But in Paderborn, behind closed doors, the prevailing mood was one of uncertainty, concern and nervousness. The company had to contend with several challenges. The dollar crisis of 1971 had thrown the European economy into recession and reduced the demand for office equipment. But the main problem was of a different nature. The 820, developed in 1965 by Otto Müller, was being overtaken by technological developments. Although it had been improved again and again, it responded no more to the needs and expectations of the customers. So far it had been possible to extend its life by making gradual improvements. But it was urgent to decide whether the time had come to draw a line and stop production.

This required the availability of a replacement that promised to be equally successful. Müller had been working on a more powerful system. The 820 featured a magnetic core memory, an integrated keyboard and a typewriter for output. He had conceived a freely programmable machine with integrated screen and cassette memory, a dot matrix printer and a module that allowed data to be transferred to higher-level computers.

But Nixdorf did not quite understand what he had in mind and paid no attention. Disappointed, Müller left Paderborn. His departure solved a human problem; Nixdorf freed himself from an oppressive dependence. By the same token he ran the risk of opening a gap that would be hard to fill. Moreover, he was confronted with personnel problems in the laboratory: Hahnewinkel, Hager and Bonatschek, instead of working as a team on a common project, tried to outdo one another, each pursuing his own ideas. Their quarrels became from day to day more intense.

In search of a new product the development department was unable to come up with, Helmut Rausch discovered that a small American company called Entrex had developed a new data collection system. Instead of using punch cards to transfer the data, the machine used magnetic tapes and magnetic discs. The device was not what he was looking for, but it promised to open up an interesting market niche.

Nixdorf entered into a licensing agreement and introduced the 620 to the market in 1973. It was an immediate success. Within a relatively short time, it reached a market share of 45 percent in Germany and of 24 percent in Europe. Nixdorf decided the time had come to take over the company and to integrate it into the computer division of Victor. In May 1974, he acquired Entrex for $22 million. His v.s. business volume suddenly increased to about 90 million dollars.

When suddenly the global economy slid into recession, demand for office equipment dropped. During the years of fast growth, the major European office equipment manufacturers, Olivetti, Philips, Ericsson, Triumph-Adler and Kienzle, had vastly expanded their production. IBM, which until then had focused exclusively on the mainframe business, had entered the market with its low-end System/32 intended to meet the needs of small and medium businesses. It all led to fierce competition for every customer.

In December 1974, Nixdorf announced the disk storage system 8870 as a successor to the system 820. It was equipped with a powerful magnetic disk storage device that revolutionized computer architecture. In addition to data collection and processing, it made stored data simultaneously available on four screens. The hardware of the 8870 consisted of a central unit in LSI technology. Its extremely large capacity, easy access and low cost of operation made it possible to efficiently track sales, orders, inventory changes and balance sheet accounts. It could be connected to four workstations.

The 8870 was the first of a new series that was gradually expanded by adding several features. It was intended for small and medium companies. In April 1975, at the Hannover Fair, Nixdorf displayed the 8870 series. Three model variants were available. They were derived from the machines whose development Müller had started in 1968.

A few days before the fair, Nixdorf had signed an agreement with a small American computer manufacturer, Digital Computer Controls Inc. The company had developed a low priced digital calculator that incorporated cutting edge technology and whose features could be adapted to improve the performance of the 8870.

The Paderborn laboratory re-engineered and restructured the machine to give it the standardized modular design and appearance that was the trademark of the Nixdorf machines. Two models, the 8870/3 and the 8870/5, were equipped with an entirely novel software program. The package could be adapted to the specific needs of each customer. It became known under the name COMET. Its components, with adaptations for more than 180 vertical markets, were sold more than 180000 times, suddenly making Nixdorf one of the major software providers in Europe.

In 1976, the development engineers completed a new banking terminal system, the 8864. It was a huge success and gave Nixdorf a dominating position, with more than 40 percent of the European market. Thus, at a time when computer technology went through its second major expansion phase, Nixdorf had a new generation of calculators ready for the market [16]

Nixdorf adopted technical innovations and brought several new products onto the market in 1974/1975: the disk-based 8870 system with multiple terminals and COMET application software, the 620 data entry system, computerized point-of-sale systems, and the 8864 banking system with terminals for the front office.

Nixdorf's success in the banking sector was founded on ambitious projects such as that with the Swedish Scandinaviska Enskilda-Bank, which networked its branches throughout Sweden with the aid of 1100 Nixdorf terminals. The product range for financial institutions was extended in 1978 with the addition of self-service systems such as statement printers and automated teller machines.

Furthermore, Nixdorf advanced to become one of the largest software companies in Germany - particularly with his COMET software package. COMET components with adaptations for more than 180 vertical markets were sold more than 100000 times. From the 1980s, international open standards prevailed in the computer market. Nixdorf followed this trend with its universal Targon system, which was based on the UNIX operating system.

On July 1, 1977, Nixdorf and his staff celebrated the 25th anniversary of the company. The turbulences of the recent past had been overcome and a new expansion phase was in progress. The slump had lasted much longer than expected and had taken its toll. But now it was over: the office equipment market had considerably improved.

From the 1980s, international "open" standards prevailed in the computer market. Nixdorf followed this trend in 1985 with the universal Targon system, which was based on the manufacturer-independent UNIX operating system.

Heinz Nixdorf and his family still owned 100% of the company stock, which gave him a decisive advantage over his major competitor Siemens, a conglomerate unable to keep up with the rapidly changing computer world. While such a concentration of ownership offered more flexibility and the ability to move quickly, it also limited the company's capital base. In 1978, Nixdorf dallied with a number of suitors eager to buy up large chunks of the corporation. But he refused to relinquish control, instead making a conditional sale of 25% of his stock to long-time ally Deutsche Bank in 1979.

In addition to his traditional strength in the small business and banking sector, Nixdorf expanded to provide information services retail companies. Nixdorf's retail involvement primarily involved point-of-sale equipment, an area in which the company became one of the European leaders. The fourth leg of Nixdorf's marketing platform was in place by 1982, when its telecommunications division created Germany's first digital telephone switching system. Heinz Nixdorf predicted that telecommunications would provide 50 percent of corporate revenue by the century's end, as the gradual convergence of telecommunication and computer systems opened a vast new field known as integrated service digital networks.

But to pursue such goals, he needed more capital. In 1984 the company made its first public offering of stock. Response was outstanding, as expected for a company whose 1984 sales had reached DM3.27 billion and continued to climb at about 21% per year.

Early in 1986, Nixdorf was more than ever optimistic about the future. On May 17, shortly before midnight, during a company party held in a circus tent at the Hannover Fair, amidst his family, his customers and friends, the band suddenly stopped. Nixdorf had suffered a heart attack and collapsed on the dance floor.

7 The Debacle

When the news of Nixdorf's death spread, his employees were stunned, wondering how the company he had managed for more than 30 years with immense success would do without him. But Nixdorf had carefully planned his succession. In the mid-seventies, he had a suffered a heart attack and considered this as a warning. He had prepared his closest collaborator, Klaus Luft, to become his successor.[17]

For several years, Luft had been in charge of sales. In 1978, he became deputy chairman and was considered Nixdorf's right hand; but had no real responsibility and no power to make any decision. He was the executive assistant of the decisions made by Nixdorf and the first to bear the brunt of anger of his boss when a problem arose.

For 20 years, he had witnessed Nixdorf being praised and hailed as an exceptional entrepreneur. He knew that whatever he did would be measured by what his former boss would have done. Not accustomed to making decisions and take responsibility, he tried to copy the man he had served for years, without having his format.

In March 1987, at the Hannover Fair, he gave a detailed explanation of his marketing strategy and of his plans for the near future. He expected to double sales over the next four to five years. So far, the main pillars of the business had been the financial institutions, the small and medium companies and - to a limited extent - the industrial corporations. He intended to become the number one in the industrial sector and expected to make substantial progress.[18]

The core business of the company was based on a system developed in 1976. It was still selling, thanks to the customer loyalty developed over the years by the company's outstanding services. But the industry was in the throes of a price war. The low-priced dollar made it difficult for German companies to export, while it was easier for the Americans and the Japanese to sell in Germany.

The electronics industry, after years of rapid growth, suffered a serious setback. Nixdorf was particularly hurt. The product line of the company was fragmented and outdated. For years, Nixdorf had led his company from success to success. He understood like no one else how to turn technical ideas into heaps of money. In 1988, for the first time in its history, sales sagged by more than 10 percent; profits dropped by 40 percent. What may have looked like a temporary accident was in fact the result of a long sales slippage due to a combination of home-made mistakes, a sudden market breakdown and increased competition.

Only through the sale of land and buildings worth about DM 250 million, was it possible to present a positive balance sheet. The era of double-digit growth rates was over. The new management that took over after Nixdorf's death was largely to blame.

Luft had promised to overtake IBM and double sales within four years. Thanks to a new line of powerful computers, the company would expand its customer base. In the United States, where despite years of struggle, little progress had been made. He was confident that sales would continue to grow and decided to hire 5000 new employees.

The errors of the past now became manifest. The core problem was that the product line was outdated and uncompetitive. IBM had launched its AS/400 intended for small and medium enterprises, a market where Nixdorf made a third of its sales. More important, the PC was becoming ever more efficient and powerful and was priced much lower the Nixdorf machines.

Luft announced an ambitious project: the programs of the computers would be updated and replaced by an operating system called Unix. It had been developed by AT&T in 1989, and included 60 commands. Several computer companies wanted to make it the standard for the entire industry. But its chances of success were uncertain. Unix was a powerful and technically advanced system that was mainly used in scientific and technological areas. It had not been successful in the commercial sector because it was expensive and difficult to program and operate. Unix would require the retraining of the sales team and the expansion of the service personnel. The conversion would cost several hundred million DM and take some time.[19]

Nixdorf had become Europe's largest producer of software and built a dedicated and knowledgeable sales force to help its customers make efficient use of the machines and programs they purchased that earned him the loyalty that ensures repeat sales. As the months went by, a rather embarrassed Klaus Luft admitted that profits would indeed not be spectacular.

Basic mistakes had been made in the days of Heinz Nixdorf who had overlooked the growing importance of the personal computer. He was convinced that he did not have to keep pace with new developments and was perfectly able do things his own way. This was a fateful miscalculation from which the company never recovered. From thereon, he was out of touch with cutting edge technology. In the mid-eighties, the trend was clearly away from entrenched mainframe and minicomputer systems toward open systems where customers were not bound by the products of a single manufacturer. Such systems featured standardized interfaces and peripheral interconnects as well as third party hardware and software. These standard devices could be produced in very large quantities and were considerably lower priced.

In Paderborn, conditions gradually deteriorated. Production methods were outdated and costly. These weaknesses had been obscured over the years by the double-digit growth of sales. In this critical time, the arrival of Klaus Luft at the head of the company proved to be disastrous.

Despite the fact that the order books listed considerably reduced entries, he refused to change his plans and to admit he was wrong. He promised the record result of the previous year would be surpassed. He sold several buildings and pieces of land the company owned. His chief accountant secretly used misleading figures to produce positive financial statements. Thanks to this, he was able to announce a profit of DM 26 million.[20]

But the company kept running further into trouble and slipped into the red. The balance sheet presented a hole of at least three quarters of a billion DM. A three decade winning streak came to an end and Luft found himself with his back against the wall. A company regarded as the ultimate of German efficiency faced an uncertain future. Quality consciousness, reliability and ingenuity were once considered its strengths; during the four years when Luft was in charge, they became a major weakness.[21]

The year 1989 proved to be an unprecedented nightmare. Losses topped DM one billion. In addition, the company suffered a triple blow from the economy at large. The price of computer chips skyrocketed; the Nixdorf mix of sales shifted rapidly from high-margin bank installations to low-margin office and retail work; increased competition and standardization of products severely depressed prices. The international movement toward open systems meant that an increasing percentage of equipment was interchangeable, which drove standard part prices down and forced competitors to "add value" to their own products in order to justify a higher selling price.

In December 1989, barely two years after earning record profits, Nixdorf Computer AG was on the edge of the abyss. The crash was obviously due to mismanagement. The man in charge, Horst Nasko, was responsible. Until recently he had been responsible for customer relations and was perfectly satisfied with his job. One Sunday morning, he received a call from Gerhard Schmidt, chairman of the supervisory committee, telling him that Klaus Luft intended to resign and that he intended to take over.

The following morning, Luft made a brief appearance at the board meeting. In a few words he announced his resignation and disappeared. His sudden departure put an end to an unusual career.

It was obvious that the new management would not be able not keep the company going and make it survive without a capable personality at the top and without a financially strong partner.

The debacle was exacerbated by the general downturn of the market. But the root causes of the decline were due to the fact that Nixdorf's successor did not understand the business nor the market.

By the mid-eighties it became obvious that the operations performed by the Nixdorf computers could be handled more efficiently and at considerably less money with personal computers.

For three and half years, Klaus Luft headed the Nixdorf Computer AG. For some time, he had been under pressure from the board of directors to resign. Given the losses the company had accumulated, it was only a matter of time before the board would react. In addition to the financial problems, he had made several errors in the product policy of the company. He had failed to recognize the importance of the open computer system that provided standard software and was making its presence felt in the world of bank data processing.

But Luft had another problem; because of his indecisiveness in taking risks, the company did not have the new products it urgently needed. Horst Nasko who replaced him was a man of different caliber. However, because of the desperate situation of the company, his job would be hazardous to carry out. The balance sheet at the end of the year 1989 turned out to be far worse than expected. The management had figured that the loss would be limited to DM 600 million. The deficit amounted to nearly one billion DM. Under these circumstances, a restoration of the company's capital structure was obviously impossible.

Shortly after taking office, he announced to the staff and to the public that the Management Board had decided to enter into a strategic partnership. Immediately several German and American companies let it be known that they were interested.[22]

Despite such problems, Siemens paid 350 million DM. The acquisition gave the company a strong position in the midrange computer market, where it was weak, and made it the seventh largest computer maker in the world. For the Nixdorf family, the deal brought to an abrupt end one of Germany's most successful postwar miracles.

8 Siemens Nixdorf

On August 23, 1990, two crucial and momentous episodes occurred in Germany. Shortly after midnight, following a heated debate at the Volkskammer of the German Democratic Republic between proponents of unification and supporters of continued independence, the president of the assembly announced that the majority had voted for reunification with the German Federal Republic.

The following morning, an extraordinary chapter of German economic history came to an end. The shareholders of the Nixdorf Computer AG met for the last time. Horst Nasko informed them that during the first half of the year, sales had dropped by 11 percent to 2.1 billion DM, and that the deficit amounted to DM 226 million. The situation was hopeless. The only way out was to accept the purchase offer made by Siemens to take over.

A few weeks later, at a board meeting held in Munich, Horst Nasko made no bones about the poor results of the past year. He called it "the most difficult in the history of the company". He blamed himself for having been too optimistic. But the main reason of the problem was the size of the company: too large for a niche market and too small to compete with the leaders of the industry. He was very optimistic about the future and looked forward to a fruitful cooperation between Munich and Paderborn.[23]

Siemens wanted a smooth transition. The Nixdorf family was to retain a portion of the shares and would have a say on the board. Nixdorf was strong where Siemens was weak: sales and service personnel were readily available and very efficient; they knew how to adapt the machines to the unique requirements of each customer. Siemens was not flexible enough to provide such service. Initially the company had produced mainframes. Not until the early eighties, when Japanese and American competitors flooded the market with inexpensive personal computers did management decide to follow the trend. Both companies would complement each other by a merger. Siemens was absent in the midrange systems where Nixdorf had a substantial market share. Nixdorf served mainly customers in the retail, banking and insurance business. Siemens supplied large companies and governmental agencies.

On October 1, 1990, the computer division of Siemens was combined with Nixdorf Computer AG. The electronics giant paid DM 350 million and acquired control of the emblematic computer pioneer. The name of the company was changed to Siemens-Nixdorf Informationssysteme AG. Siemens held 91 percent of the capital and occupied the key positions in the supervisory and the executive board. Siemens' chief strategist Franz Hermann was named chairman.

A maverick entrepreneur was swallowed up by a much larger competitor it had outperformed in the marketplace. The merger brought together two completely different worlds. For both it meant a culture shock and a sudden fracture with the past. Nixdorf was a flexible company, oriented to the needs of its customers. Siemens was a huge self-centered bureaucratic corporation. For both a new and turbulent phase began in the computer industry.

On the face of it, the merger made sense and was by far the best possible solution: the synergy potential was obvious. The former flagship had become a failure. It not only made Siemens the last-minute savior of a former competitor; it enhanced its position in the global computer market. But the merger was not without risk. Siemens took over an ailing company burdened with huge losses. The last financial year had ended with a deficit of nearly one billion DM. Without giving up its independence, Nixdorf Computer AG would have been bankrupt within a few months. After the merger, drastic remedial measures would be needed. Massive job cuts were unavoidable. And because of the different corporate cultures, friction was to be expected. [24]

The Siemens management had considerably underestimated the problems that would result from the acquisition of an ailing company, and the difficulties involved in amalgamating and coordinating the functioning of two very distinct operating methods and styles. Siemens' management had conceived a bookkeeping operation that would offset the losses incurred by Nixdorf against the profits earned by its computer division. But the combined operation soon ran into unexpected financial problems due in part to the sudden breakdown of the global computer market.

The appointment of the board of directors led to controversy: it was extremely difficult to co-ordinate the accounting methods of both companies. Disagreements arose about the sharing of responsibilities between Paderborn and Munich.

The situation was aggravated by the fact that the personnel of the two companies found it very difficult to communicate. The Nixdorf people complained about Siemens' heavy bureaucracy, used to dealing with large companies and unable to understand the needs of small and medium businesses. At Siemens, they scoffed at the careless manner in which the Nixdorf contracts were formulated. Instead of two signatures, they only bore the sign of one manager. Although the slogan "Synergy at Work" had been widely advertised in large-format ads, in practice there was little evidence of it. All too often the personnel of both companies worked side by side but not together. After a while, several Nixdorf top people decided to quit. The new company took some time to re-organize internally. In order not to antagonize anybody, chief positions were filled twice; product lines that should have been scrapped were continued.

Nixdorf's customer base was ten times larger. When visiting the offices in the Spanish, French and Dutch subsidiaries to verify the accuracy of the financial statements, the Siemens auditors uncovered accounting irregularities and unusually large personal expense accounts. Some customers had paid far less for their machines than the price shown on the catalog. The number of company cars was not justified; sudden promotions and salary increases had been granted shortly before the merger. Such situations could be corrected; but it would very difficult to turn the two companies into a unified operation. A new product alone would not solve the problems.[25]

Very soon Siemens' management realized that it was facing huge problems. Although the merger produced the largest computer manufacturer in Europe, it was doubtful that it would work out in the foreseeable future.

In fact, three years after the merger, Siemens was looking for a partner. Renamed Siemens Nixdorf Informationssysteme (SNI), the association soon floundered. Some observers had predicted that Siemens' acquisition was doomed from the start. This was largely due to Nixdorf's overemphasis on the micro-computer market. While this market had been one of the major sectors in the computer industry in the 1980s, by the early 1990s it had become largely obsolete, crushed by the rise of the personal computer and the by development of efficient networking systems. [26]

9 Portrait of the Man

Drawing by Konrad Zuse

For much of the postwar era, Nixdorf epitomized the Wirtschaftswunder, Germany's extraordinary recovery from the devastation of war. During his lifetime, he became a legend as the visionary young entrepreneur who had the nerve to challenge the giants of the industry. He started out with a moped, a few hand tools and a project. He set up his workshop in the basement of an electric power plant and built it into a one-man global company employing 24000 people. In 1986, at the age of 60, during a company party at the Hannover Fair, he was struck by a heart attack.

He had a project and turned it into a fabulous success. The idea of bringing the computer to the office was in complete contrast to the strategy of the industry leaders. Yet he prevailed, and thereby opened up a whole new market.

The technical knowledge acquired through years of hard work, allowed him to recognize with incredible foresight the value of new ideas and to put them into practice faster than anyone else. The fact that he was exceptionally successful had many causes. Above all, he had a sure touch that gave him the ability to identify opportunities as they presented themselves. He had the extraordinary ability to reduce complex matters to the simplest possible denominator and to concentrate on what was really important. This allowed him to have a clear view of the potential. Once he made a decision, he went ahead regardless the consequences.

He had the sixth sense which gave him the self-confidence to do the right thing at the right moment and to choose the right man at the right time. He recognized and amply rewarded individual merit. He praised and promoted as long as it served his purpose. He also abruptly parted with anyone who was no longer suitable for the job or no more willing to devote himself to the company with the same devotion he demanded of himself. He had no time for superfluous sentimentality: he alone decided what was needed. He set his goal and anyone who wanted to achieve that goal with him had to be prepared to work for it or resign.

He had the courage to take risks, self-confidence, a pioneering spirit, discipline and motivation to venture into untested waters. He regarded work as his mission in life, but also as an opportunity to play a part in the shaping of society. He considered the creation of jobs as one of the most important responsibilities of an entrepreneur.

He had the rare gift of being able to think in simple terms. Instead of being tempted to devise complex solutions to the problems he encountered, his intuitive grasp of the essential issues and his ability to gain insights from them always led him to practice-oriented results.

He paved the way for decentralized data processing. For this, he conceived and created computers that were easy to operate. He held patents, but was not an inventor. He was the entrepreneurial designer of practical technical solutions, manufacturing methods and marketing strategy. He was a social individual. He established institutions and benefits for his employees that were far more generous than was common at the time.

Konrad Zuse and Heinz Nixdorf

Nixdorf wanted his company to remain independent. He set up two non-profit foundations: the Heinz Nixdorf Stiftung and the Stiftung Westfalen were established to hold the shares in Nixdorf Computer AG. After the takeover of Nixdorf Computer by Siemens AG in 1990, these foundations pursued their varied non-profit-making mission. He was both a visionary technician and a businessman. He had an intuitive understanding of corporate finances and quickly grasped the key figures in the balance sheets of his foreign subsidiaries. He was both a visionary technician and a businessman. He had an intuitive understanding of corporate finances and quickly grasped the key figures in the balance sheets of his foreign subsidiaries.

Nixdorf tended to be outspoken, which did not always go down well. His overriding interest was the welfare of his fellow human beings. The image of Heinz Nixdorf as a model social entrepreneur continues to live on in the memories of those that were close to him. Nixdorf was an optimist, convinced he could overcome any obstacle. His leadership style and the organizational structure of his company were based on the idea that victory belongs to the bold.

He provided his employees with the best possible working conditions and made sure that everyone got a chance. He was generous, but gave away nothing. Employees who enjoyed his trust were granted great freedom of action and personal responsibility. He particularly valued the foremen and the highly skilled workers for their expertise, commitment and their sense of responsibility.

He was an unusual executive in that he was not only the manager, but owned the business lock, stock and barrel. When Fortune Magazine selected the ten best managers in Europe, he ranked number one. But he did not care for hype. He preferred to live quietly with his family in an inconspicuous flat roof bungalow that was also the headquarters of the company.[28]

His commanding style impressed those who came in contact with him and was readily accepted by the personnel. But he kept everyone at a distance. Nobody would have dared call him by a nickname.

Heinz Nixdorf possessed all the characteristics of a dynamic entrepreneur: the willingness to take risks, self-confidence, a pioneering spirit, discipline and motivation. He regarded work as his life's mission, but also as an opportunity to take part in the shaping of society.

As a computer pioneer, he paved the way for decentralized data processing. He envisioned and created computers that were intended to be easy-to-operate tools for the workplace: Even in his later years, he was able to dismantle and reassemble computers during factory tours for visitor groups; the demonstration never failed to astonish.

Whenever he had the occasion to speak his mind publicly, he used to get excited about two issues in particular: both the government subsidies and Siemens. In 1985, the Bonn Ministry of Research and Development approved a DM 20 million grant for a collaborative research project. For the first time, he cooperated with his favorite enemy.[29]

He was a social individual in the best sense of the word. He established social institutions and benefits for his employees that were far more generous than was common at the time. Nixdorf wanted his company to remain independent; it should certainly not be subject to control from third parties. Thus the two non-profit foundations, the Heinz Nixdorf Stiftung and Stiftung Westfalen, were established to hold shares in Nixdorf Computer AG. After the takeover of Nixdorf Computer by Siemens AG in 1990, these foundations pursued their varied nonprofit-making goals.

He was exceptionally competent with corporate finances, and could grasp the key figures in the balance sheets of foreign subsidiaries or business partners more quickly than many experts.

He held patents of his own, but was not a typical inventor. He was the entrepreneurial designer of practical technical solutions, manufacturing methods and distribution processes. He was both a visionary technician and a businessman.

He was convinced that an entrepreneur does not gain legitimacy by the wealth he accumulates, but by the contribution he makes to society. He loathed bureaucrats; in his view, they are an unproductive crowd. He could occasionally be aggressive. He tested his power by challenging the giants of the industry. The accumulation of wealth was not the driving force in his life. It touched a key experience of his early years: the loss of his father and the privations his mother, brothers and sisters had to endure. The memory of these hardships never left him.

The introduction of the company's shares on the stock exchange in June 1984 put the financial structure of the company on a secure basis. He set up two non-profit foundations: The purpose of the Heinz Nixdorf Stiftung was the promotion of research and teaching in the field of science, with emphasis on information technology. It is also meant to prevent that one day the company could be shaken by a power struggle within the family. The Stiftung Westfalen was intended to contribute to the health of the personnel. Both were intended to make sure the Nixdorf Computer AG would remain independent and secure.

-NB – All pictures courtesy of Nixdorf ComputerMuseumsForum

Notes

1   K. Kemper. *Heinz Nixdorf. Eine deutsche Karriere*. Verlag Moderne Industrie AG. 1986. pp. 27-30.

2.   Kemper, K. pp. 35-47.

3.   Kemper, K. pp. 55-68.

4.   Kemper, K. pp. 78-96

5.   *Nixdorf zwischen MDT und IBM*. Computerwoche Nov. 6, 1987.

6.   K. Kemper, pp. 110-115.

7.   K. Kemper, pp. 127-151.

8.   K. Klemper, pp. 85-106.

9.   *Rechner für Amerika*. Computerwoche, Oct. 7, 1968.)

10.   *Eine deutsche Erfolgsstory*. Computerwoche. Nov. 13, 1987.)

11.   *Rein bei Entrex, raus by Amdahl*. Computerwoche,   May 27, 1977.

12.   K. Kemper, pp. 104/105.

13.   Computerwoche, Sept 25, 1988.

14.   *Nixdorf: Im Kleinen Gross*. Der Spiegel, March 15, 1971.

15.   K. Kemper, pp.85-106.

16.   K. Kemper, pp. 124-126.

17.   *Irgendwie ein Leitbild*. Der Spiegel, March 24, 1986.

18.   *Nixdorf will weiter wachsen*. Computerwoche, March 13,1987.

19.   *Von Oben herab*. Der Spiegel, April 4, 1988.)

20.   *Nixdorf: Ohne Partner Chancenlos*. Der Spiegel, Dec. 12, 1989.

21.   *Schnell veralted*. Der Spiegel, Nov. 20, 1989.

22.   *Luft-Nachfolger Nasko tritt schweres Erbe an*. Computerwoche, Dec. 1, 1989.

23.   *Nixdorf-Ohne Partner Chancenlos*. Der Spiegel, 25 Dec. 1989.

24.   *Siemens Nixdorf: Schlimmer Einbruch*; Der Spiegel, July 15,1991.

25. *Erst mal verdauen*. Der Spiegel, Sept 19, 1991.
26. *Tödlicher Kulturschock*. Handelsblatt, Oct. 6, 2006.
27. *Die Firmen-Jäger*. Der Spiegel, April 3, 2000.
28. *Der Knorrige Patriarch der Elektronik*. Die Zeit, August 10, 1948.
29. *Nixdorf kooperiert mit Siemens*. Der Spiegel, Nov. 4, 1985.

After a brief stint as a lawyer, Armand Van Dormael was for 25 years in charge of the European buying offices of Sears Roebuck. Having lived through several monetary crises, he decided to take early retirement and study monetary history. His first book, **Bretton Woods: Birth of a Monetary System** remains a worldwide bestseller. **The Power of Money** relates the collision between sovereign states and international financial powerhouses for the control of global finance.

In 2012, he published **The Silicon Revolution**. The book traces the theoretical foundations of computer science and the pioneering break-throughs made by German and French scientists that led to the invention of the transistor and of the microcomputer.

After completing the manuscript, he realized that he had overlooked Heinz Nixdorf, one of the most important and fascinating personalities in the history of computing, As a student, he realized that most companies could not afford a mainframe, but needed small and versatile computers tailored to their needs.

He set up his workshop in the basement of an electric power plant and built it into a one-man company employing 24000 people and producing one percent of the global computer industry, with a cash flow of 4.5 billion DM a year. In 1986, at the age of 60, during a company party held at the Hannover Fair, he was struck by a heart attack.

For much of the postwar era, Nixdorf epitomized the *Wirtschaftswunder*, Germany's extraordinary recovery from the devastation of war.

During his lifetime, he became a legend as the visionary young entrepreneur who had the nerve to challenge the giants of the industry.

The Heinz-Nixdorf MuseumsForum is the largest computer museum in the world. It presents the latest computer applications and technologies, and attracts over 100000 visitors a year.

www.ingramcontent.com/pod-product-compliance
Lightning Source LLC
Chambersburg PA
CBHW061034050326
40689CB00012B/2816